VIRGIN ISLANDS
NATIONAL PARK

by Ruth Radlauer

Photographs by
Ed and Ruth Radlauer and
Henry M. Anderson

Design and map by
Rolf Zillmer

AN ELK GROVE BOOK

CHILDRENS PRESS ™

CHICAGO

With special thanks to the park naturalists who make any national park more meaningful.

Photo credits:
Henry M. Anderson, all underwater photographs except as noted below
Dr. Al Hibbs, pages 5 (blue angelfish), 15 (Christmas tree worm)
National Park Service, pages 17, 25 (snorkeler), 39 (weaving)

Glossary, page 41 by courtesy of Lito Valls

Cover: Coral—Tubastrea Aurea

Library of Congress Cataloging in Publication Data

Radlauer, Ruth Shaw.
  Virgin Islands National Park.
  (Parks for people)
  "An Elk Grove Book."
  SUMMARY: Discusses the animal life, vegetation, and history of the national park in the Caribbean Sea.
  1. Virgin Islands National Park—Juvenile literature. 2. St. John, Virgin Islands—Juvenile literature. 3. Natural history—Virgin Islands of the United States—Virgin Islands National Park—Juvenile literature. [1. Virgin Islands National Park. 2. National parks and reserves]
  I. Radlauer, Edward. II. Anderson, Henry M. III. Title.
  F2098.R32   917.297'22   80-22457
  ISBN 0-516-07741-4

3 4 5 6 7 8 9 10 11 12 13 14 15 R 91 90 89 88 87 86 85

Contents

What is Virgin Islands National Park?

Virgin Islands National Park is on a green island washed by the blue waters of the Atlantic Ocean and the Caribbean Sea. It's a lush green forest of plants nourished by warm sun and rain. And it is an underwater wonderland.

This park is plants. On hikes with naturalists, you will get to know the red hibiscus, the pink gushee-gushee, and the haiti-haiti tree. You may even get to crunch on some tasty fresh coconut or slurp a juicy papaya.

At Virgin Islands National Park, you will find beautiful beaches covered with white sand. You'll swim in warm waves that lift you on their way to shore. Here you can even learn to snorkel. Then you can watch colorful tropical fish darting in and out among the coral reefs.

The United States bought the islands of St. Thomas, St. Croix, and St. John from Denmark in 1917. In 1956, about two-thirds of St. John was made a national park. Now it's a place where visitors can enjoy changing seascapes, marine life, and coral gardens.

Trunk Bay

Red Hibiscus

Blue Angelfish

Your Trip to Virgin Islands

Plan ahead to make your trip to Virgin Islands National Park more fun. You can learn to snorkel in rented gear at the park. But if you take snorkel lessons at home and bring your own gear, you'll have more time to swim among the fish and coral. The tropical sun burns even while you swim, so take a T-shirt to shield your skin.

Hiking trails call for boots or walking shoes and a sun hat. You also need rain gear and an insect repellent. On a seashore walk, you need old tennis shoes so you can wade over sharp things.

To get to this park, you go by plane or ship to the island of St. Thomas. From there a twenty-minute ferry ride brings you to Cruz Bay on St. John. Then it's only a short walk to the Visitor Center. Here you can get a map and a schedule of park activities. Visitors who plan to stay need a taxi, bus, or rented car to get to the campground.

Write to Cinnamon Bay Campground, Box 720, St. John, Virgin Islands 00830, to reserve a tent site, tent, or cottage. For a free park map and information, write to the Superintendent, Box 7789, St. Thomas, Virgin Islands 00801.

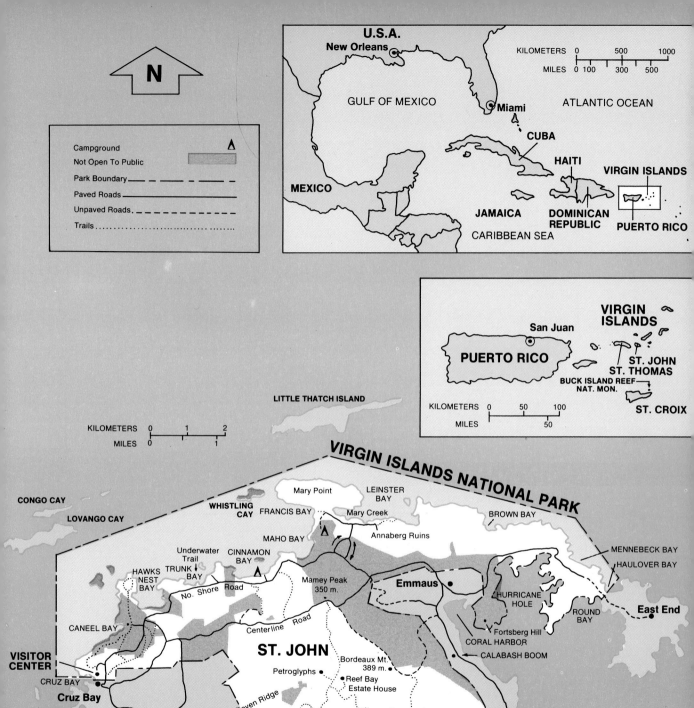

N

Legend

Campground
Not Open To Public

Park Boundary
Paved Roads
Unpaved Roads
Trails

U.S.A.
New Orleans

KILOMETERS 0   500   1000
MILES 0 100 300   500

GULF OF MEXICO

ATLANTIC OCEAN

Miami

CUBA

HAITI

VIRGIN ISLANDS

MEXICO

JAMAICA

DOMINICAN
REPUBLIC

PUERTO RICO

CARIBBEAN SEA

VIRGIN
ISLANDS

San Juan

PUERTO RICO

ST. JOHN
ST. THOMAS

BUCK ISLAND REEF
NAT. MON.

ST. CROIX

KILOMETERS 0   50   100
MILES   50

LITTLE THATCH ISLAND

KILOMETERS 0   1   2
MILES 0   1

VIRGIN ISLANDS NATIONAL PARK

CONGO CAY

LOVANGO CAY

WHISTLING
CAY

Mary Point

LEINSTER
BAY

FRANCIS BAY

Mary Creek

BROWN BAY

MENNEBECK BAY

HAULOVER BAY

MAHO BAY

Annaberg Ruins

HAWKS
NEST
BAY

Underwater
Trail

CINNAMON
BAY

TRUNK
BAY

No. Shore Road

Mamey Peak
350 m.

Emmaus

HURRICANE
HOLE

ROUND
BAY

East End

CANEEL BAY

Centerline   Road

ST. JOHN

Fortsberg Hill

CORAL HARBOR

CALABASH BOOM

VISITOR
CENTER

Bordeaux Mt.
389 m.

CRUZ BAY

Petroglyphs

Reef Bay
Estate House

Cruz Bay

Seven Ridge

Lameshur

Johns Folly

TURNER BAY

FISH
BAY

Sugar Mill
Ruins

JOHNS
FOLLY
BAY

LEDUCK ISLAND

GREAT CRUZ BAY

REEF BAY

CHOCOLATE
HOLE

RENDEZVOUS
BAY

EUROPA BAY
GREAT LAMESHUR BAY

DRUNK BAY

Salt
Pond

GROOTPAN BAY

SALT POND
BAY

Ram
Head

Anemone, bryzoan, coral. Are these the ABC's of "sea talk?" When you go on a guided seashore walk or snorkel with a park naturalist, you may hear some strange words. They are the language of *marine biology.*

"A *sea cucumber* is an *echinoderm*."

"*Fire coral* is a *hydroid* with cells that sting."

From *alga* to *zebra ark,* sea talk sounds like another language, but here are a few words you may want to know.

Sea Talk

alga	water plant (seaweed) which has no true roots, stems, leaves, or flowers—Algae are grouped according to color.
anemone	flowerlike animal—Its tubular body is a sac with a mouth surrounded by tentacles.
barnacle	crustacean that attaches itself to rocks and other hard things and gathers food with feathery legs
blue tang	small, sky-blue fish with a spine near its tail
brain coral	hard coral with a surface that looks like a brain
brittle star	animal with five thin arms similar to a seastar
bryzoan	marine invertebrate that attaches itself to hard surfaces and grows in mosslike colonies, giving it the appearance of a plant
calcium carbonate	material taken from sea water by some sea animals such as corals to form a hard protective cover or skeleton
chiton	mollusk with a jointed shell of eight overlapping plates and a muscular foot used to attach to rocks
cling fish	tiny, lizardlike fish with suctioned fins on its underside—It clings to rock and coral.

...ral	tubelike animals called polyps that grow in colonies attached to each other—The polyps of hard corals form outer skeletons. Polyps of soft corals have inner skeletons and soft outsides.
...hinoderm	group of sea animals with lumpy or spiny skin; includes seastar, sea cucumber, sea urchin
...l grass	underwater grass plant with long narrow leaves
...khorn coral	hard coral that looks like an elk's antlers
...e coral	not a true coral but an animal closely related to the jellyfish—It grows on hard surfaces and looks smooth, but has cells that sting and cause a burning rash in humans.
...nge reef	coral reef formed next to shore
...orgonian	soft coral with a branching skeleton inside the soft outer polyps
...ouper	large fish that spends its early life as a female and later becomes a male
...unt	small fish that makes a grunting sound and travels in a school
...ermit crab	small crustacean that lives in another animal's empty shell—As it grows, it must throw off one shell and find a bigger one.
...droid	group of animals with stinging cells, often mistaken for plants (seaweed)
...vertebrate	animal without a backbone
...nd crab	large edible crab that lives in holes on land
...npet	mollusk with a cone-shaped shell
...ng spine sea urchin	black sea urchin with very long, brittle, barbed spines
...arine biology	the study of plants and animals that live in salt water
...ollusk	soft-bodied invertebrate—Some have shells and some do not. They include clams, conch, octopus, and others.
...ursery	place where young are born and grow big and strong enough to take care of themselves

photosynthesis	process by which plants use light, water, and carbon dioxide to produce food—In the process, plants give off oxygen.
plankton	tiny plant and animal life floating or swimming in water
polyp	the living part of coral which secretes the hard skeleton
predator	animal that catches and kills other animals to eat
reef	ridge at or near the surface of water—In Virgin Islands, reefs are formed by coral and coralline algae.
rock-boring sea urchin	spiny round animal that scrapes grooves in rocks and dead coral as it eats algae
school	many fish of one kind swimming in a group as a means of defense
sea cucumber	echinoderm that lives on the ocean floor and eats sand in order to digest microscopic plants and animals growing on sand particles
sea egg	West Indian name for a white sea urchin
sea slug	sea *nudibranch*
sea star	starfish
seaweed	large branching alga
snail	mollusk with a soft body inside a shell
soldier crab	land hermit crab that finds an empty shell by the seashore to wear for protection
symbiosis	relationship between two living things in which each benefits from the other
tentacles	tubelike arms of corals and anemones armed with stinging cells
turtle grass	similar to eel grass—These underwater plants form nursery areas for many forms of sea life.
vertebrate	animal with backbone and bony skeleton, including fish, mammals, birds, reptiles, and amphibians
zebra ark	a common, two-shelled (bivalved) mollusk with striped shells
zooxanthellae	small alga cells that live within coral in a symbiotic relationship—The alga is well protected from predators and the coral receives oxygen from the alga's photosynthesis. See *symbiosis*.

The Reef-Corals

More than anything, this park is an underwater wonderland to explore. Around the islands are reefs, underwater formations made out of millions of living and dead corals.

A coral is a mass of limestone formed by millions of little tubelike animals called polyps. Each polyp attaches itself to a hard surface. Its body gives off calcium carbonate which hardens into a casing around the lower half of its body. A flat sheet of tissue connects the middles of many polyps and they become a colony called a coral.

At night the polyps reach out of their casings. At the soft end of each polyp are tentacles around a mouth. The tentacles gather tiny plants and animals called plankton from the water. The plankton is then passed into the polyp's mouth and digested.

Corals get their color from microscopic algae growing in the polyps. Corals also get oxygen from algae. Algae are plants that get carbon dioxide (CO_2 for short) from the polyps. The algae combine CO_2 with water and sunlight to produce plant cells. As algae do this, they give off the oxygen that coral must have to live.

Corals—Tubastrea Aurea

Coral Polyps

Brain Coral

The Reef- Anemones and Sponges

Corals grow very slowly, and are always being destroyed by pollution, animal activities, and wave action. Snorkelers who stand on corals damage them. And one drop of a boat anchor can break off years of a coral's growth.

But even dead corals are important to the reef. They form a base on which all kinds of plants, animals, and other corals live.

"Flowers of the sea," anemones, cling to rocks and dead corals. Their tentacles reach out for tiny fish and one-celled animals. These tentacles sting and paralyze their prey. Then they pass the prey toward the mouth at the center of the anemone's body.

Anemones can move a little from day to day, but a sponge must stay in one place. A sponge is a soft animal that may be round or shaped like a basket or crooked fingers. Through small holes all over its body, a sponge pumps water in and filters food out of it. Then it passes the water out through different, bigger holes. A sponge must filter about one ton of water to get enough food to gain one ounce of body weight.

Anemone

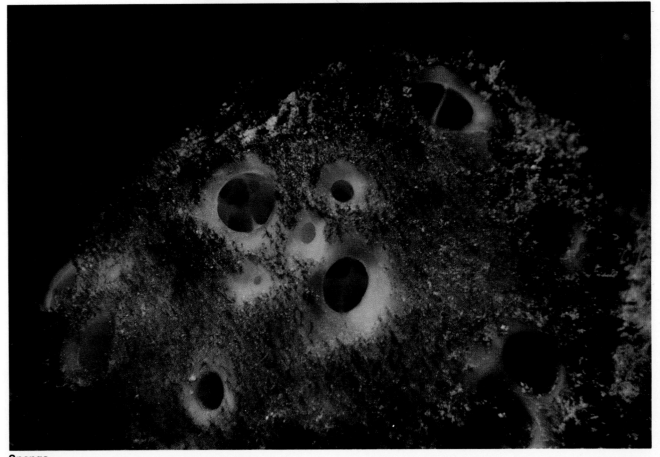

Sponge

Christmas Trees and Feather Dusters

Swaying and bobbing in the water around the reef are some other strange creatures. They may look like flowers, but they're really worms and sea squirts.

The Christmas tree worm looks like a spiraled flower as its tentacles reach out to gather food. If you touch it, the "flower" disappears into a drab tube that you wouldn't even notice. Later, it blossoms out as it was before you disturbed it.

A feather duster worm behaves in much the same way. Its white tube is made of the same material as sea shells.

Sea squirts live on rocks, seaweeds, loose sediments, and soft corals. They can be shaped like cylinders or like globes. A sea squirt sucks tremendous amounts of water into and through itself as it filters food out of the water. When disturbed, the sea squirt violently contracts its body and squirts water.

All of these animals, along with corals, anemones, and sponges, make the reef a wonderland full of surprises.

Christmas Tree Worm

Feather Duster Worm

Sea Squirt

The Web of Life

In water, as on land, there is a web of life that begins with plants. In the ocean, a food chain begins with algae, plants with no true roots, stems, leaves, or flowers. You can see some algae, but you would need a microscope to see most of them. These tiny plants, along with some microscopic animals, are called plankton.

Plants store the sun's energy in their cells which become food for plant eaters. Fish and other sea animals filter plankton out of sea water as it passes through their bodies. Plant eaters are eaten by other animals, which are then eaten by bigger animals. This is a food chain that carries the energy of the sun through plants to the animal world. As bodies of dead animals decay and become food for plants, the chain begins again. There are many food chains in nature, and they are woven together in a "web of life."

Careless building, reckless boating, and water pollution can easily disturb the web of life on the reef. Workers in the park try to show us how to protect the web in Virgin Islands National Park.

A Web Of Life

Adult French Angelfish

Fish

Fish of the coral reef are different from those in deeper waters. They're smaller and need warm water to live. Some, like the butterfly and angel fishes are very colorful. You may see a banded butterfly or blue tang when you snorkel at Trunk Bay.

Predators, like the grouper, prey on other fish. This keeps a balance between fish and the food supply because the grouper removes weak and injured fish.

Different species of fish have interesting ways to protect themselves. Grunts live in groups called schools. By moving in close formation, a fish is less likely to be taken by a predator. Schools may break up at night, but they regroup in the morning or when a predator comes along.

The cowfish protects itself with its bony skeleton. It can also secrete a strong poison that kills other fish.

A spiny puffer's defense is to fill itself with water. Then its spines stand out and it becomes a prickly thing to swallow.

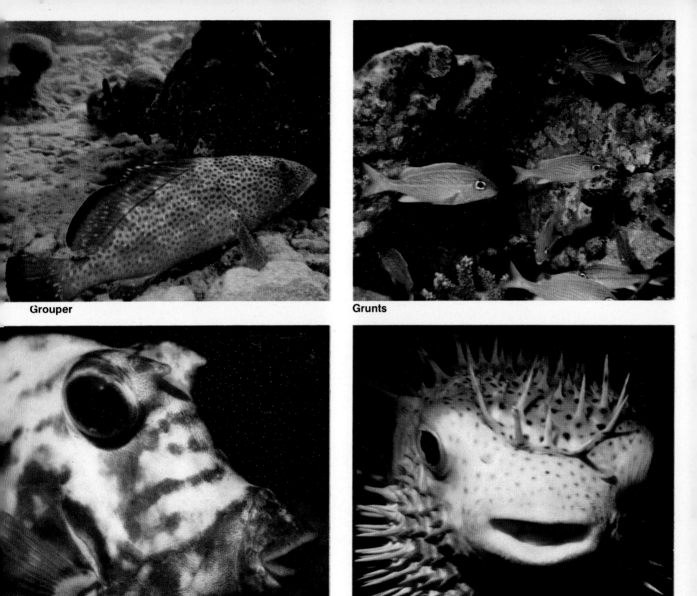

Grouper

Grunts

Cowfish

Spiny Puffer

Life on a Rock

On a guided walk with a naturalist, you can discover thousands of life forms. In your old tennis shoes, you wade into shallow water along the shore.

The naturalist may pick up a rock or piece of dead coral to see what creatures cling to its underside.

It's impossible to count them, and nothing is what it seems to be. You think you see moss, but it's really algae growing on a shell. A pink crust looks like a mineral deposit, but it's an alga.

Maybe you'll find a kind of mollusk called a chiton. This animal is an invertebrate, which means it has no backbone. The chiton's soft body is enclosed in a segmented, or jointed, shell of eight overlapping plates. It grips a rock and scrapes off algae for food. Other mollusks on the rock might be snails, limpets, or sea slugs.

You may see a brittle star, a very fast-moving relative of the sea star. If a predator grabs the brittle star by one of its five arms, the arm can break off. The star escapes and goes on about its business of feeding on the sea floor and growing a new arm.

Life On A Rock

Algae Growing On A Shell

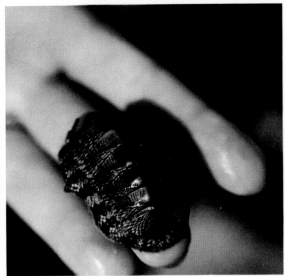

Chiton

Brittle Star

Other Weird Things

On the same rock, you may see the rock-boring sea urchin. As the naturalist turns it over, you see five teeth at its center. With these five strong teeth, the sea urchin makes grooves as it scrapes algae from the rocks.

After you inspect all this life on a rock, the naturalist is careful to put it back exactly as it was found. If the rock is left wrong side up, the animals could die from exposure to sun, dry air, and predators.

As you wade, you may find another weird animal called the sea cucumber. Its skin is rough but not spiny like the sea urchin's. Sea cucumbers feed by eating sediment, the sand and silt on the ocean floor. They take sand particles into their bodies and digest the bacteria and microscopic algae that grow on each grain of sand.

A sea cucumber defends itself from predators by turning inside out. It shoots out all its insides, including the stomach. While the predator inspects these, the sea cucumber crawls away to a safer place. Like the sea star and other echinoderms, this animal can regrow parts of its body.

Rock-Boring Sea Urchin

Find Sea Cucumbers On A Seashore Walk

To Know the Sea

By wading at the seashore, you first get to know the sea. Then on a guided snorkel tour, the sea becomes your friend.

Before you snorkel, the park naturalist makes sure you know how to use your equipment. Then he or she tells about the fish and corals you're going to see. You learn that none of the fish will hurt you. "But stay away from fire coral!" she says. "This smooth, mustard-colored animal is not a true coral, and you can get a burning rash if you brush against it. Also, watch where you put your hands and feet so you won't get a barb from the spiny sea urchin."

Once in the water, you can hardly believe the strange shapes and waving branches you see. You bob up and down and watch blue tangs, sergeant majors, and banded butterfly fish. When you pass a school of grunts, you hear, "Uh, uh." And what are those clicking sounds? Pebbles knocking together? Shrimp snapping their pinchers?

As you get to know the sea, you relax and begin to feel like a fish yourself. When this happens, you know you're ready to go with a buddy to the self-guided underwater trail at Trunk Bay.

Guided Seashore Walk, Rain Or Shine

Snorkel Instruction

Relax And Be A Fish

The Island

How do you build an island with reefs where people like you can explore? You start about 100 million years ago with a volcano at the bottom of the sea. In thousands of eruptions and millions of years, volcanoes poured many layers of lava onto the bottom of the Caribbean Sea. During these years, the earth rose very slowly and pushed the mounds of lava above the water. The islands of St. John and St. Thomas were born!

Again, volcanoes exploded, and for thousands of years more, lava spewed out to make the islands bigger and higher. Eruptions stopped about 60 million years ago, but earth movements continued. Cracks in the crust formed peaks and valleys.

As soon as an island forms, erosion and weathering start to carve at it. Heavy rainfall washes down bits and pieces of the peaks. These bits settle as sediment along the shore and in the surrounding sea. When the water is clear and warm, corals grow and form reefs. They make a fringe around the edge and the island continues to grow.

An Island From Lava? ▶

Plants

You might wonder how these mounds of lava became a green paradise. At first wind, water, and migrating birds brought seeds and spores to the islands. Sun, rain, and rich volcanic soil did the rest. The seeds grew into flowering plants, grasses, and trees. Spores produced mosses and ferns.

The mangrove tree was brought by water. Mangrove seedlings sprout while still on the tree. A seedling then drops into the water. It can float hundreds of miles until it lands on a sandbar or island. Then it takes root and grows. A year later, it sends out prop roots that make it strong enough to stand against strong wind and waves.

Oysters and fish begin life among mangrove prop roots. This tree is also a land builder. Its roots trap sand, sticks, grass, and leaves. The debris decays and becomes soil which is held in place by the mangrove tree.

Many species of trees covered St. John Island until people cut them down to make room for sugar cane and other crops. Most of the forest you see in the park today has grown since the end of sugar cane farming.

Mangrove Trees ▶

Your "Terrarium"

Snorkeling on the reef is like diving into a giant aquarium. And hiking the trails of St. John is like walking through a huge terrarium.

This "terrarium" has a balanced ecosystem. Animals breathe in oxygen and give off carbon dioxide (CO_2). Plants need CO_2 to carry on a process called photosynthesis. Trees, bushes, ferns, and flowers use the sun's energy to combine CO_2, water, and nutrients from the soil. The result is the green cells of which plants are made.

During photosynthesis, plants give off oxygen which animals need to live. As you can see, plants and animals provide each other with gases to breathe. And of course, many animals, such as lizards and rodents, eat plants and get eaten by other animals.

Droppings and dead bodies of animals decay and add nutrients to the soil. Plants need these nutrients as well as the CO_2 given off by this decaying animal matter.

You can explore the ecosystem of a dry desert "terrarium" on the Salt Pond Hike. And the Cinnamon Bay Hike goes through a wet forest "terrarium."

Plants Give Off Oxygen—Passion Flower

Animals Give Off Carbon Dioxide—Anole Lizard

Cactus Grows In Dryer Places

To Know the Island

As soon as you get to the park, sign up to go on the guided Reef Bay Hike. Then you'll get to know the island's plants, animals, and history.

You'll hear how some plants were used as foods and medicines. Perhaps you'll count the legs on a gongolo worm. Maybe you'll see termites doing their job of eating dead wood and turning it into soil.

Halfway down the trail, everyone stops for lunch at the petroglyphs. These are figures carved into the rocks near a waterfall. No one is sure who carved the petroglyphs. Experts doubt they were done by Indians. Some think one or two figures could have been done by slaves during the rebellion of 1733.

One figure looks like the African Ashanti symbol meaning, "Accept God." An expert on ancient writing says the symbols look like some found in Libyan tombs in Africa dated about A.D. 150. He says they mean, "Plunge in to cleanse and dissolve away impurity and trouble." It goes on to say the water is for ceremonial washing before devotion.

This hike ends with a tour of the Reef Bay Sugar Factory and a boat ride to Cruz Bay.

Reef Bay Hike

Count The Legs On A Gongolo Worm

Petroglyphs—Plunge In . . .

Early People

The mystery of the petroglyphs makes it hard to say who were the first people of St. John. We do know the Arawak Indians came here from South America in about A.D. 300. The peaceful Arawaks came in huge canoes carved from kapok trees. They brought tools for fishing and farming and seeds for crops.

In their canoes, they may have brought a large rodent used for food. They also caught sea turtles, iguanas, and birds to add meat to their diet.

After about 1000 years, the Arawaks were chased away by the Caribs. Moving north from South America, the Caribs invaded the islands, killed and ate the Arawak men, and captured the women.

On his first voyage, Columbus discovered some of the islands now known as the West Indies. He explored further on his second voyage and found others. Some of the islands, he named the Virgins in honor of the 11,000 virgins of St. Ursula.

By this time, there were no people living on what is now St. John. There were only lush green forests soaking up the rain and sun. And tangled vines crept silently through the valleys.

Which Early People Carved Petroglyphs?

Indian Stone Pestle

Days of Rum and Sugar

The quiet of St. John was shattered in the 1700's when people from Denmark settled here. With the help of slaves brought from West Africa, they built estates and grew sugar cane and cotton. In sugar mills built of field stones, bricks, and brain coral, the Danes produced sugar and rum.

Among the slaves were people of the proud, warlike Amina tribe. They were forced to do field work, something they'd never done in their homeland. In 1733, the slaves revolted. It took eight months and the help of French and English colonists from other islands to stop the rebellion.

To keep the slaves from rebelling again, the Danes tried to scare the "unfree" with laws that called for cruel punishments. There was an uneasy peace between as many as 2000 slaves and only a few estate owners.

By 1848, many slaves had escaped. The Governor feared a rebellion on St. Croix, so he freed all the slaves in the Danish West Indies.

Without a source of free labor, the sugar estate days of St. John began to decline.

Base of Windmill—Annaberg Ruins

Brain Coral Used For Building—Annaberg

On Their Own

With the decline of the sugar industry, most of the estate owners left St. John. But as former slaves, the freed people had no place to go. They stayed and lived off the land, on their own.

Sometimes in the park today, you can see demonstrations of the ways those people survived. They made fish traps, brooms, and hats from the native teyer palm tree.

Their food included pigs, goats, guavaberries, bananas, coconuts, and the native papaya. They grated cassava root into meal and washed it to remove the sap. Then they dried the meal to make a flat waferlike bread.

Many plants were used to make medicines. Aloe vera healed burns and soothed sunburn. A heated leaf of the painkiller tree, placed on swollen joints, made them stop hurting. Besides giving a delicious fruit, the mammee apple tree provided a gummy juice from its bark. Mixed with powdered seeds, the juice was rubbed on to remove insects and chiggers from the skin.

Listen carefully on your guided walks. You may learn of a good way to cure your next toothache!

Teyer Palm

Fish Trap

Will It Be A Hat Or Basket?

To Know the People

St. Johnians are hard-working, friendly people. You will find them even more friendly if you remember some of the manners many of us have forgotten in the rush of mainland city life.

A St. Johnian likes to greet each person and chat awhile before "getting down to business." When you go into a store, you always say, "Good morning" or "Good afternoon" or "Good night" (not "Good evening"). *Then* you can say, "Where's the mustard?" or "Do you have any socks?"

It's also best not to wear a swimsuit into town. And women in shorts make St. Johnians feel uncomfortable.

Mainlanders may have trouble understanding some of the St. Johnians. People here speak a Creole English with an interesting accent. And they sprinkle their speech with some Spanish and French.

Here are a few Creole expressions to help you understand and know the people of St. John.

A Few Creole Expressions

(From a glossary by Lito Valls of St. John.)

good!	serves you right
yoh	all of you (like ''y'all'' in southern U.S.)
nen keba	It is finished. (Used for perfect agreement.)
ack-back	reverse
ack-back de beel	reverse the car
gasse	cane trash, megasse
zadee	light-headed, crazy, stupid
g eye	greedy, takes the biggest piece
oo	brother
ban	mattress, sleeping pad
shee	to have money to spend—''He so cashee, he buyin'ever't'ing.''
t style	to show off, dress smartly
clare	A plant is said to declare when it bears flowers the first time.
rbell	a ringing in one's ears—Local belief is that one's ears ring when one is being talked about.
heh!	(voice dropped at end) aha; sound of approval
ver tea	any bush tea taken to help fever pains, sometimes made of yellow cedar
r true	without question, decidedly
rty-eleven	many (not 30-11 or 50-11, but 40-11)
am	(pronounced gomm) oh my goodness
shee-gushee	small sensitive plant with pink flower; leaves fold when touched
aiti-haiti	the maho tree; has heart-shaped leaves
rd back	strong and healthy
mbug up	to bother
gone	goodbye
jumbee, jumbie	ghost, apparition, spirit, usually bad; from African Bantu
jumbee beads jumbie beads	red seeds from a vine, used as jewelry
lala	nonsense, also tall, also gossip
lang tung	person who gossips
malasi	molasses
marina	undershirt, now usually cotton, made in old days from merino, a fine Spanish wool
nebuary mont'	never
one-room mout'	person who speaks his/her mind
press hair	straightened hair
rumfle up	to disturb or throw into disorder
santa santa	hesitate, dillydally
sensey fowl	a chicken with ruffled feathers
shagray	embarrassed, surprised
sweeten	to flatter
tan tan	aunt
today day	this very day
tolian love	In trying to get attention from each other, boys and girls throw pebbles at one another. This is called tolian love.
ton-ton	1. sweetheart 2. plant, nothing nut
tuku tuku	sound imitating an engine
tuny	small, tiny
tutu	horn made from a conch shell
upstairs house	two-story house
wimpish	shy
yaba yaba	senseless chatter
zamba	small wooden bed

Jumbee Trees and Love Plants

The slaves had stories to explain things in nature. One story told why a crab walks sideways. Another gives you a good reason not to step on a spider.

Even today, some of the slaves' great-grandchildren believe the kapok is a jumbee tree. Maybe it's because bats pollinate the kapok, and bats are thought to be jumbees during the day.

One story says if you walk past a kapok tree after dark, the jumbee who lives there will turn into a bat and follow you home. The only way to keep it from coming inside is to throw out a handful of corn or rice, before it reaches the door. The jumbee has to count all the kernels before it can come in. You try to throw out enough to keep the jumbee counting until dawn because it must return to the kapok tree before sunrise.

The love plant, bryophyllum, tells about true love. A young woman writes the name of the man she loves on a leaf of bryophyllum. She plants the leaf, and if it grows, the man is sure to return her love. The love plant will grow almost anyplace, so the bryophyllum usually makes everyone happy.

Kapok Tree—Jumbee Tree?

Love Plant—Bryophyllum

To Know the Earth

A smiling person greets you at the Visitor Center and says, "Welcome. Come and stay awhile. Browse around and get to know us. Take your time, because if you hurry, you might miss something in your national park."

To know Virgin Islands National Park is to know the sea, the reef, the land, and the people. Let the naturalists introduce you. Then linger and look, listen, smell, taste, and touch.

Touch a sea whip and watch it fold into itself. Or touch the gushee gushee and see its leaves fold in. Taste a guavaberry or genip fruit. Smell the bark of a cinnamon tree and a leaf of the bay rum. Knock on the trunk of the fast-growing papaya tree and hear its hollow sound. Be lazy and listen to the lap lap of waves as they wash the sand beneath a sunset sky.

Think about the island and how it formed. Remember the fish hiding among the corals. Ponder the web of life on land and sea.

While you're at it, imagine a terrarium as big as the world. Could it be that to know Virgin Islands National Park is to know the earth?

Take Time

Don't Miss A Thing

Bequest of Beauty

Each national park is a BEQUEST OF BEAUTY, a gift for those who follow. It is a place of special interest or beauty that has been set aside by the United States Government especially for you, your children, and their great-great grandchildren. This bequest is yours to have and to care for so that others who follow can do the same during their lives.

The Author and Illustrators

Wyoming-born Ruth Radlauer's love affair with national parks began in Yellowstone. During her younger years, she spent her summers in the Bighorn Mountains, in Yellowstone, or on Casper Mountain.

Ed and Ruth Radlauer, graduates of the University of California at Los Angeles, are authors of many books for young people. Along with their adult daughter and sons, they photograph and write about a wide variety of subjects ranging from monkeys to motorcycles.

The Radlauers live in California where Ruth and Ed spend much of their time in the mountains near Los Angeles.

At an early age, Henry M. Anderson discovered in books that an underwater world awaited him. His intense interest in the sea led him to graduate as a marine biologist from the University of North Carolina at Wilmington.

Henry Anderson was a park naturalist at Virgin Islands National Park and is now at Cape Hatteras National Seashore. His wife Gail is also a marine biologist. With their two children, they enjoy snorkeling and taking pictures under water. Except as noted on page 2, all the underwater photographs in this book are by Henry Anderson.